An Ideal Husband

OSCAR WILDE

Level 3

Retold by Mary Gladwin
Series Editors: Andy Hopkins and Jocelyn Potter

Pearson Education Limited
Edinburgh Gate, Harlow,
Essex CM20 2JE, England
and Associated Companies throughout the world.

ISBN: 978-1-4058-6236-3

First published by Penguin Books 2002
This edition published 2008

1 3 5 7 9 10 8 6 4 2

Text copyright © Penguin Books Ltd 2002
This edition copyright © Pearson Education Ltd 2008
Illustrations copyright © Richard Gray 2002

Typeset by Graphicraft Ltd, Hong Kong
Set in 11/14pt Bembo
Printed in China
SWTC/01

Published by Pearson Education Ltd in association with
Penguin Books Ltd, both companies being subsidiaries of Pearson Plc

For a complete list of the titles available in the Penguin Readers series please write to your local
Pearson Longman office or to: Penguin Readers Marketing Department, Pearson Education,
Edinburgh Gate, Harlow, Essex CM20 2JE, England.

Contents

Introduction

LORD CAVERSHAM: *Why do you like London Society so much? It's full of nobodies talking about nothing.*
LORD GORING: *I love talking about nothing, Father. It's the only thing I understand.*
LORD CAVERSHAM: *You seem to live only for fun.*
LORD GORING: *Why not? What's more important, Father?*

An Ideal Husband is one of Oscar Wilde's most popular plays. It is both amusing and thoughtful. Everything happens in about forty hours, some time in the early 1890s, beginning with a party at the lovely London home of Lord and Lady Chiltern.

The main characters are all rich and well known. Some of the women are beautiful and bored. They are interested only in fine clothes and other people's lives. Others are more serious. Some of the men hold important government positions. Others, like Lord Goring, only want to enjoy themselves. They go to dinner parties and to the theatre almost every night. They are always polite and amusing and they never talk seriously.

But one woman has learned a secret which gives her power over other people. She says that she will tell it to the world. Who will stop her? How? And who will get hurt?

Here we discover another side of the characters. They become interested in ideas. They discuss questions of right and wrong. They want to do the right thing, but at the same time they want to be happy. What should they do? It is difficult for them to decide. And what will other people think? They must always follow the rules of London Society.

An Ideal Husband was written in England in 1895. English society is of course very different now. And today people around the world can read this play in their own languages. The characters speak and act differently from the people that we know. But we can still understand the problems of the people in the play. And we can still enjoy reading and discussing it.

Oscar Wilde was born in Dublin, Ireland, in 1854. His father was a doctor and a writer. His mother wrote Irish political poems. He studied at Trinity College in Dublin (1871–4), and the University of Oxford (1874–8). He wrote the poem *Ravenna* while he was at Oxford, then a book of poems in 1881.

At Oxford, Wilde met other writers. They believed that art and beautiful things were very important in life. In 1882, Wilde travelled around America and made speeches about these ideas. Then, in London, he gave speeches about American society.

Wilde married an Irish woman, Constance Lloyd, and they had two sons. Wilde wrote two books of children's stories for them: *The Happy Prince and Other Tales* (1888) and *A House of Pomegranates* (1892).

Wilde was very successful in the 1890s. He wrote *The Picture of Dorian Gray* in 1891. Then he wrote four amusing plays about London Society: *Lady Windermere's Fan* (1892), *A Woman of No Importance* (1893), *An Ideal Husband* (1895) and *The Importance of Being Earnest* (1895). These plays were immediately very famous and popular. People liked them because Wilde used language very cleverly. They could laugh at their own society and at themselves. Wilde also wrote a serious play, *Salomé*, in 1893. The British government stopped him showing this play in London. It was first acted in Paris in French.

Oscar Wilde belonged to the part of London Society that he wrote about. He loved art, music, fine clothes and good conversation. He also liked to be different from other people. He made many enemies and was sent to prison for two years. When he came out he was poor and ill. He could not write in England, so in 1897 he went to live in Paris. In 1898 he wrote *The Ballad of Reading Gaol* about life in prison. He died in Paris in 1900.

Reading and acting the play

You can read *An Ideal Husband* silently, like every other story in a book. You will have to imagine the places, the characters' clothes and their voices from the pictures and the words on the page.

But *An Ideal Husband* was written for actors on a theatre stage. You can read the play in a group with other people. This is very different from silent reading because you can bring the characters to life. They can sound happy, sad or angry. You can add silences and important noises, like the sound of ringing for a servant. You can also stop and discuss the play. What does this character mean? Why does he or she say that?

You can have more fun if you act the play. There are party scenes, and scenes with just two people. The characters can show their feelings by their words, but also on their faces and by their actions. If you act *An Ideal Husband*, the rooms and houses should look different. You should also think about stage equipment – the letters, the brooch, the chairs and sofas, the desk. Some characters have large parts, like Sir Robert and Lady Chiltern, Lord Goring and Mrs Cheveley; others, like the servants, only have a few short lines. Many of the guests at the Chilterns' party don't speak. How many guests do you need?

An Ideal Husband is a wonderful play. You can read it or you can act it. But have fun and enjoy it!

The Characters in the Play

LORD CAVERSHAM, a rich man, about seventy years old

LORD GORING, Lord Caversham's son, thirty-four, handsome and well dressed

PHIPPS, one of Lord Goring's servants

SIR ROBERT CHILTERN, forty, dark-haired, dark-eyed and good-looking. He has a strong, intelligent face, but he looks nervous and tired. He works for the British government, in the Foreign Office.

LADY CHILTERN, Sir Robert's wife, a beautiful, serious woman, about twenty-seven

MISS MABEL CHILTERN, Sir Robert Chiltern's pretty sister

MASON, one of the Chilterns' servants

JAMES, one of the Chilterns' servants

MRS CHEVELEY, a tall, red-haired woman

LADY MARKBY, a pleasant, kind woman, with grey hair and fine clothes

LADY BASILDON, a very pretty young woman

MRS MARCHMONT, a very pretty young woman

PARTY GUESTS (who do not speak)

Act 1 A Surprise Guest

Scene 1

[*A very big room at Sir Robert and Lady Chiltern's house. Lady Chiltern is greeting party guests. Mrs Marchmont and Lady Basildon are sitting together on a sofa.*]

MRS MARCHMONT: Are you going to the Hartlocks' tonight, Margaret?

LADY BASILDON: I think so. Are you?

MRS MARCHMONT: Yes. They give terribly boring parties, don't they?

LADY BASILDON: Terribly boring! I don't know why I go. I never know why I go anywhere.

MRS MARCHMONT: I come here to learn from people.

LADY BASILDON: Ah! I hate learning!

MRS MARCHMONT: I do too. But, dear Gertrude, Chiltern always says, 'You need a serious purpose in life!' So I come here to find one.

MASON [*calling the name of a new guest*]: Lord Caversham.

[*Lord Caversham walks into the room.*]

LORD CAVERSHAM: Good evening, Lady Chiltern! Has my good-for-nothing young son been here?

LADY CHILTERN [*smiling*]: I don't think Lord Goring has arrived yet.

MABEL CHILTERN [*coming up to Lord Caversham*]: Why do you call Lord Goring good-for-nothing?

LORD CAVERSHAM: Because he's so lazy.

MABEL CHILTERN: How can you say that? He goes horse-riding at ten o'clock in the morning, changes his clothes at least five times a day and goes out every night.

1

LORD CAVERSHAM [*looking at her kindly*]: You're a very charming young lady!

MABEL CHILTERN: And you are very sweet, Lord Caversham! Please come and visit us more often.

LORD CAVERSHAM: I never go anywhere now. I'm sick of London Society.

MABEL CHILTERN: Oh, I love it! Half the people are beautiful and stupid. And the other half are intelligent and crazy.

LORD CAVERSHAM: Oh! Which is Goring?

MABEL CHILTERN [*seriously*]: Lord Goring is different from other people. But he's changing nicely!

LORD CAVERSHAM: Into what?

MABEL CHILTERN [*smiling*]: I hope to tell you very soon, Lord Caversham!

MASON [*calling*]: Lady Markby, Mrs Cheveley.

Scene 2

[*Lady Markby and Mrs Cheveley walk in.*]

LADY MARKBY [*to Lady Chiltern*]: Good evening, dear Gertrude! Thank you for inviting my friend, Mrs Cheveley. Two charming women like you should meet.

LADY CHILTERN: [*She smiles and moves towards Mrs Cheveley, then suddenly stops smiling.*] I think Mrs Cheveley and I have met before. I knew her by another name. Has she married a second time?

LADY MARKBY [*pleasantly*]: Ah, people marry as often as they can. Marriage is very popular now, isn't it?

MRS CHEVELEY: But have we really met before, Lady Chiltern? I have been out of England for a long time.

LADY CHILTERN: We were at school together, Mrs Cheveley.

MRS CHEVELEY: Really? I have forgotten all about my schooldays. I think I hated them.

LADY CHILTERN [*coldly*]: I'm not surprised!

MRS CHEVELEY [*sweetly*]: I'll be happy to meet your clever husband, Lady Chiltern. He has become famous since he joined the Foreign Office. The newspapers in Vienna talk about him all the time.

LADY CHILTERN: What will you and my husband talk about, Mrs Cheveley? I can't imagine!

[*She moves away. Sir Robert comes in.*]

SIR ROBERT: Good evening, Lady Markby. Who is this charming person you have brought to us?

LADY MARKBY: Her name's Mrs Cheveley. She has just arrived from Vienna. I'll introduce you.

SIR ROBERT [*pleasantly*]: Everyone wants to meet the charming Mrs Cheveley.

MRS CHEVELEY: Thank you, Sir Robert. I'm sure that we will become real friends. And now can I walk through your beautiful house? I hear your paintings are charming. Poor Baron Arnheim told me about them.

SIR ROBERT [*surprised*]: Did you know Baron Arnheim well?

MRS CHEVELEY [*smiling*]: Yes, very well. Did you?

SIR ROBERT: Yes, a long time ago.

MRS CHEVELEY: He was a wonderful man, wasn't he?

SIR ROBERT [*after a few seconds*]: He was very ... unusual.

MASON [*calling*]: Lord Goring.

[*Lord Goring comes in.*]

SIR ROBERT: Good evening, my dear Arthur! Mrs Cheveley, this is Lord Goring. He's the laziest man in London.

MRS CHEVELEY: I have met Lord Goring before.

LORD GORING [*smiling*]: Do you still remember me, Mrs Cheveley?

MRS CHEVELEY: Yes, of course. My memory is excellent.

LORD GORING: Are you staying in London long?

MRS CHEVELEY: I haven't decided. I'll stay if the weather and the cooking are good. I also have to talk to Sir Robert.

[*She smiles at Lord Goring and goes out with Sir Robert. Lord Goring goes over to Mabel Chiltern.*]

MABEL CHILTERN: You're very late!

LORD GORING: Have you missed me?

MABEL CHILTERN: Terribly!

LORD GORING: Then I'm sorry I didn't stay away longer.

MABEL CHILTERN: How very selfish of you!

LORD GORING: I *am* very selfish.

[*Lord Caversham comes up to his son.*]

LORD CAVERSHAM: Well, sir! Why aren't you in bed? I heard that you were dancing at Lady Rufford's the other night until four o'clock in the morning!

LORD GORING: Only a quarter to four, Father.

LORD CAVERSHAM: Why do you like London Society so much? It's full of nobodies talking about nothing.

LORD GORING: I love talking about nothing, Father. It's the only thing I understand.

LORD CAVERSHAM: You seem to live only for fun.

LORD GORING: Why not? What's more important, Father?

LORD CAVERSHAM: You're heartless, sir, very heartless!

LORD GORING: I hope not, Father.

[*Lord Caversham joins the other guests.*]

MABEL CHILTERN: Lord Goring, will you take me to dinner?

LORD GORING: I'd love to, Miss Mabel.

[*They leave the room and the other guests follow.*]

Scene 3

[*Sir Robert and Mrs Cheveley come in.*]

SIR ROBERT: And are you going to any of our country houses before you leave England, Mrs Cheveley?

MRS CHEVELEY: Oh, no! I hate your English house-parties. People try to be interesting at breakfast. But *you* will decide if I stay in England, Sir Robert. [*She sits down on the sofa.*]

SIR ROBERT [*sitting next to her*]: Seriously?

MRS CHEVELEY: Quite seriously. I want to talk to you about the Argentine Canal Company.

SIR ROBERT: What a boring subject for you, Mrs Cheveley!

MRS CHEVELEY: Oh, I like boring subjects, but I don't like boring people. You're interested, I know, in international canals. You were Lord Radley's secretary, weren't you? The government put money into the Suez Canal at that time.

SIR ROBERT: Yes, but England needed the Suez Canal. The trip to India became shorter. But this Argentine Canal is criminal! It's just a way to make money!

MRS CHEVELEY: It's business, Sir Robert! A brave plan.

SIR ROBERT: Believe me, Mrs Cheveley, it's criminal. We have a report on it at the Foreign Office. People have put money into the Canal, but the work hasn't begun. Nobody knows where the money is. I hope that you haven't put money into it. I'm sure you are much too clever.

MRS CHEVELEY: I have put a *lot* of money into it.

SIR ROBERT: Who gave you that idea?

MRS CHEVELEY: Your old friend – and mine. Baron Arnheim.

SIR ROBERT [*thinking*]: Ah! Yes. I remember that he wanted the Canal. I heard that at the time of his death. [*standing up*] But you haven't seen my paintings. Can I show them to you?

MRS CHEVELEY [*shaking her head*]: I don't feel like looking at paintings. I want to talk business.

5

SIR ROBERT: I'm afraid that I cannot help you, Mrs Cheveley. You should put your money into something safer. The Argentine Canal will not be successful if England is against it. I'm going to speak about the report in the House* tomorrow night.

MRS CHEVELEY: You must not do that, Sir Robert. That will not help me or you.

SIR ROBERT [*looking at her in surprise*]: Me? My dear Mrs Cheveley, what do you mean?

MRS CHEVELEY: Sir Robert, I'll be quite honest with you. I do not want you to give the report to the House. You must say that the information in it is wrong. Say that the government is thinking about the international importance of the Canal. If you do that, I'll pay you very well!

SIR ROBERT: Pay me! You can't be serious.

MRS CHEVELEY [*speaking slowly and clearly*]: I'm quite serious. You're a man of the world. Everybody has a price.

SIR ROBERT [*angrily*]: I'll call your carriage for you. You have lived abroad too long, Mrs Cheveley. Don't forget that you are talking to an Englishman!

MRS CHEVELEY [*putting her hand on his arm*]: I remember exactly who I'm talking to. I know how you made your money. You sold a government secret to a businessman! And I have your letter too.

SIR ROBERT: What letter?

MRS CHEVELEY: The letter that you wrote to Baron Arnheim. You were Lord Radley's secretary then. You told the Baron to put his money into the Suez Canal. Three days later, the government agreed to put money into it.

SIR ROBERT: The Suez Canal was only a plan then. The government agreed to it later.

*(Commons): One of the two houses of the UK Parliament

'I know how you made your money. You sold a government
secret to a businessman!'

MRS CHEVELEY: Your action was criminal, Sir Robert. And now I'm going to sell you that letter. This is the price: You must make a speech in the House. Tell everyone that the Argentine Canal is a good plan. You made money out of one canal. You must help me and my friends to make money out of another!

SIR ROBERT: But I can't do that. It's wrong!

MRS CHEVELEY: You mean you can't say no. If you refuse . . .

SIR ROBERT: What then?

MRS CHEVELEY: I'll go to your English newspapers. I'll tell them this story and give them the letter. And they will destroy you! Before I leave you tonight, you must give me a promise. You will stop your report. And you will say that the Argentine Canal plan is a good idea.

SIR ROBERT: I can't! [*in a low voice*] I'll give you any sum of money you want.

MRS CHEVELEY: You can't buy back your past, Sir Robert. Even *you* haven't got enough money. Nobody has.

SIR ROBERT: I will not do what you ask me.

MRS CHEVELEY: You must decide now. I have got to send a message to Vienna tonight. [*She moves towards the door.*]

SIR ROBERT: Don't go. I agree. I'll stop the report.

MRS CHEVELEY: Thank you. I'm glad that we have agreed. And now you can get my carriage for me, Sir Robert. I see that people have finished dinner.

[*Sir Robert leaves.*]

Scene 4

[*Lady Chiltern, Lady Markby, Lord Caversham, Lady Basildon, Mrs Marchmont, Lord Goring and Mabel Chiltern come in.*]

LADY MARKBY: Well, dear Mrs Cheveley, I hope you have enjoyed yourself. Sir Robert is very amusing, isn't he?

MRS CHEVELEY: Most amusing! I have enjoyed my talk with him very much.

LADY MARKBY: He has done excellent work in the government. And Lady Chiltern is a wonderful example for us all. And now I must go, dear. Good night.

MRS CHEVELEY: Good night.

LADY MARKBY [*to Lady Chiltern*]: Good night, Gertrude!

[*She goes out holding Lord Caversham's arm.*]

MRS CHEVELEY: What a charming house you have, Lady Chiltern! I have spent a lovely evening. Your husband is so interesting.

LADY CHILTERN: Why did you want to meet my husband, Mrs Cheveley?

MRS CHEVELEY: Oh, I wanted to interest him in the Argentine Canal plan. He didn't agree with it before. Most men don't listen, but he did. I changed his mind in ten minutes. He's going to make a speech in the House tomorrow. We must go and hear him! It will be a great day!

LADY CHILTERN: I'm sure you have made a mistake. My husband is against the plan, so he will never agree.

MRS CHEVELEY: Oh, but he has. My trip here has been a great success.

SIR ROBERT [*returning*]: Your carriage is here, Mrs Cheveley!

MRS CHEVELEY: Thanks! Good evening, Lady Chiltern! Good night, Lord Goring!

MRS CHEVELEY: Will you take me to the door, Sir Robert? We have the same interests now, so we will be great friends.

[*She goes out holding Sir Robert's arm. Lady Chiltern watches them. Then the other guests join her and they go into another room.*]

Scene 5

[*Lord Goring and Mabel Chiltern are alone.*]

MABEL CHILTERN: What a terrible woman! [*She sees something lying on the sofa.*] What's this? Someone has dropped a brooch!

LORD GORING: It's a handsome bracelet.

MABEL CHILTERN: It isn't a bracelet. It's a brooch.

LORD GORING: It can be a bracelet too. [*He takes it and calmly puts it in his pocket.*]

MABEL CHILTERN: What are you doing?

LORD GORING: Miss Mabel, I have a strange request.

MABEL CHILTERN [*interested*]: Oh, please ask! I have waited for it all evening.

LORD GORING [*a little surprised*]: Don't tell anybody that I have taken this brooch. If someone asks for it, write to me.

MABEL CHILTERN: That *is* a strange request.

LORD GORING: Well, you see, I gave this brooch to somebody, years ago.

MABEL CHILTERN: You did?

LORD GORING: Yes.

[*Lady Chiltern comes in alone. The other guests have gone.*]

MABEL CHILTERN: Then I'll say good night. Good night, Gertrude! [*She leaves.*]

LADY CHILTERN: Good night, dear!

Scene 6

LADY CHILTERN [*to Lord Goring*]: Did you see the person who Lady Markby brought here tonight?

LORD GORING: Yes. It was an unpleasant surprise. What did she come here for?

LADY CHILTERN: She wanted to talk to Robert. She wants him to help her with that dishonest Argentine Canal plan.

LORD GORING: She has chosen the wrong man, hasn't she?

LADY CHILTERN: Yes. She can't understand an honest man like my husband!

LORD GORING: But clever women sometimes make surprising mistakes. Good night, Lady Chiltern!

LADY CHILTERN: Good night!

[*Sir Robert comes in.*]

SIR ROBERT: How beautiful you look tonight, Gertrude!

LADY CHILTERN: Robert, it's not true, is it? You don't agree with this Argentine Canal plan, do you? You can't!

SIR ROBERT [*surprised*]: Who told you about that?

LADY CHILTERN: That woman who has just gone out. She calls herself Mrs Cheveley now. Robert, I know this woman and you don't. We were at school together. She told lies all the time and she was a thief. Why do you listen to her?

SIR ROBERT: Gertrude, we must not judge people by their pasts.

LADY CHILTERN: But what did she mean? Are you going to help her with that Argentine Canal plan? You say it's dishonest.

SIR ROBERT [*uncomfortably*]: I made a mistake. I have changed my mind. We can all make mistakes.

LADY CHILTERN: But you told me about the report yesterday. It's against the plan.

SIR ROBERT [*walking up and down*]: My men got the wrong information. I have changed my mind. That's all.

LADY CHILTERN: All! Oh, Robert! This is a terrible question, but have you told me everything?

SIR ROBERT: Why are you asking me a question like that?

LADY CHILTERN [*after a minute*]: Why aren't you answering it?

SIR ROBERT [*sitting down*]: Gertrude, it's a difficult question. And political life is a very difficult business. If you accept help from somebody, then you have to pay. Sooner or later every politician has to do that.

LADY CHILTERN: Everyone? Robert, why are you talking so differently tonight? Why have you changed?

SIR ROBERT: I haven't changed. But things have changed.

LADY CHILTERN: But your ideals can't change!

SIR ROBERT: But sometimes it's necessary.

LADY CHILTERN: Dishonesty can never be necessary, Robert. What will it give you? Money? We don't need it! Power? Power is no good if you use it badly. It's dishonest!

SIR ROBERT: Gertrude, you must not use that word. It's for political reasons. I told you that.

LADY CHILTERN: Robert, other men can give up their ideals, but you can't. You're not the same as other men. You have always been an example to the world and to me. I love you because you are perfect. If you change, then I'll lose my love for you. And if I lose my love, I'll lose everything.

SIR ROBERT: Gertrude!

LADY CHILTERN: Robert, have you got a dark secret in your life? Tell me, tell me immediately, so . . .

SIR ROBERT: So?

LADY CHILTERN [*very slowly*]: So I can go away.

SIR ROBERT: Go away?

LADY CHILTERN: That's the right thing to do.

SIR ROBERT: Gertrude, there are no secrets in my past.

LADY CHILTERN: I knew it, Robert, I knew it. But why did you say those terrible things? You will write to Mrs Cheveley, won't you? Tell her that you can't help her.

SIR ROBERT: I'll go to see her.

LADY CHILTERN: You must never see her again, Robert. A man like you must never talk to a woman like her. No, you must write to her immediately. Tell her that you will not change your mind!

SIR ROBERT: But it's so late. It's almost twelve.

LADY CHILTERN: That's not important. Write to her, Robert. You will not agree to her plan because it's dishonest. Yes, write the word dishonest. She knows what that word means. [*Sir Robert sits down and writes. His wife picks up the letter and reads it.*] Yes, that's good. [*She rings for the servant as he writes the envelope. Mason comes in.*] Send this letter to Claridge's Hotel immediately. We do not expect an answer. [*Mason goes out. Lady Chiltern puts her arms around her husband.*] Robert, I feel that I have saved you from a danger tonight. Political life is finer and more honest today because of you. Do you realize that? I know it, and I love you for that.

SIR ROBERT: Oh, love me always, Gertrude, love me always!

LADY CHILTERN: I *will* love you always. You will always be the most honest of all men.

[*She kisses him and goes out. Sir Robert walks up and down, then sits with his face in his hands. Mason comes in and he looks up.*]

SIR ROBERT: Put out the lights, Mason, put out the lights!

[*Mason puts out the lights and the room becomes almost dark.*]

Act 2   Old Secrets

Scene 1

[*In the sitting room at Sir Robert's house. Lord Goring is sitting in an armchair wearing evening clothes. Sir Robert is walking up and down nervously.*]

LORD GORING: My dear Robert, this is very difficult. Why didn't you tell your wife everything last night?

SIR ROBERT: Arthur, I couldn't tell my wife. She's the only woman I have ever loved. If I tell her everything now, she will hate me.

LORD GORING: Is Lady Chiltern perfect?

SIR ROBERT: Yes, my wife is perfect.

LORD GORING: What a pity! I'm sorry, Robert. I didn't mean that. But I would like to talk to Lady Chiltern.

SIR ROBERT: You can try, but she will never change her mind.

LORD GORING: Why didn't you tell her years ago?

SIR ROBERT: When? When I asked her to marry me? She agreed to marry an honest man. She didn't know where my money came from. But my actions didn't hurt anybody.

LORD GORING [*looking at him seriously*]: Only yourself, Robert.

SIR ROBERT: I made a mistake eighteen years ago. I came from a good family, but I was young and poor. If people find out about it now, it will finish me! Is that fair, Arthur?

LORD GORING: Life is never fair, Robert.

SIR ROBERT: Every successful man today needs money. I fought for it and I won. Many other rich men have done the same thing. I wanted my success when I was young.

LORD GORING: Well, you are still young and you are very successful. You are only forty and you have an important position in the Foreign Office. Isn't that enough for you?

SIR ROBERT: And if I lose it now, what will I do?

LORD GORING: Robert, why did you sell yourself for money?

SIR ROBERT [*excitedly*]: I didn't sell myself for money. I bought success at a high price. That's not the same thing.

LORD GORING [*seriously*]: Yes, you paid a very high price for your success. But where did you get the idea?

SIR ROBERT: Baron Arnheim.

LORD GORING: Baron Arnheim! Tell me everything.

SIR ROBERT [*sitting down heavily in an armchair*]: I met the Baron at Lord Radley's one night. After dinner, he was talking about success in modern life. 'Anybody can be successful,' he said. 'You need power and money. Those are the most important things in life. And only rich men have power over other men and power in the world.' He was right. Money has given me great power. It has also made me free.

LORD GORING [*carefully*]: You don't believe that, do you?

SIR ROBERT [*standing up*]: I believed it then and I believe it now. You can't understand – you have never been poor.

LORD GORING: But what did the Baron want from you?

SIR ROBERT: When I was leaving he said to me, 'If you give me any useful secret information, I'll make you a very rich man.' Six weeks later I received some important papers ...

LORD GORING [*looking at the floor*]: Government papers?

SIR ROBERT: Yes.

LORD GORING [*looking up sadly*]: I'm surprised at you, Robert. Why were you so weak?

SIR ROBERT: Weak? I had to be strong and brave. I sat down that afternoon and wrote to Baron Arnheim. That woman has my letter now. Baron Arnheim made seven hundred and fifty thousand pounds as a result of it.

LORD GORING: And you?

SIR ROBERT: The Baron gave me a hundred and ten thousand.

LORD GORING: That wasn't much for what you did, Robert.

SIR ROBERT: That money gave me what I wanted. I went into the House immediately. I had power over others. The Baron sometimes helped me in business and I was successful.

LORD GORING: But tell me, Robert, did you ever feel sorry for your actions?

SIR ROBERT: No. Many other men have done the same thing. I fought and I won.

LORD GORING [*sadly*]: Do you still think that you won?

SIR ROBERT: I don't know. [*after a long silence*] Arthur, do you hate me?

LORD GORING [*sadly*]: I'm very sorry for you, Robert.

SIR ROBERT: I have never felt sorry. But I *have* given away a lot of money to the poor.

LORD GORING: To the poor? Was that really a good idea? Well, I'll try to help you if I can.

SIR ROBERT: Thank you, Arthur. But what can we do?

LORD GORING: Well, you can't tell the world that you made a mistake. People will never listen to you again.

SIR ROBERT: You're right, Arthur, I must fight it.

LORD GORING [*standing up*]: I agree. I was waiting for you to say that, Robert. First, you must tell your wife everything.

SIR ROBERT: No, I will not do that.

LORD GORING: Robert, believe me, you are wrong.

SIR ROBERT: I can't do it. She will stop loving me. But what about this woman, this Mrs Cheveley? How can I defend myself against her? You knew her before, Arthur, didn't you?

LORD GORING: Yes.

SIR ROBERT: Did you know her well?

LORD GORING: Not very well. I asked her to marry me. But I changed my mind after three days.

SIR ROBERT: Why was that?

LORD GORING [*smiling*]: Oh, I forget. It's not important now. But have you tried money? She always loved money.

SIR ROBERT: I offered her any sum she wanted. She refused.

LORD GORING: So the rich haven't got all the power.

SIR ROBERT: No. Arthur, I'm afraid that I'm going to lose everything. What can I do?

LORD GORING [*hitting the table*]: Robert, she's a danger to you. You must fight her any way that you can.

SIR ROBERT: But how?

LORD GORING: I don't know. But everyone has a weak point. Perhaps she has a secret that she wants to keep.

SIR ROBERT: I'll send a message to Vienna. Perhaps they know something about her that I can frighten her with.

LORD GORING: Oh, Mrs Cheveley is a very modern woman. She probably enjoys it when people find out her secrets.

SIR ROBERT [*writing*]: Why do you say that?

LORD GORING: Because she likes people to notice her. Did you see the dress she wore last night?

SIR ROBERT [*ringing for the servant*]: Yes, but I'm still going to ask Vienna about her.

LORD GORING: Ask the question. But don't expect an answer.

[*Mason comes in.*]

SIR ROBERT [*putting a letter into an envelope and carefully closing it*]: Send this to Vienna immediately.

MASON: Yes, Sir Robert. [*He takes the letter and goes out.*]

SIR ROBERT: I'll fight her to the death. But I don't want my wife to know.

LORD GORING [*strongly*]: Even if your wife finds out, you must fight her.

SIR ROBERT [*sadly*]: But if my wife finds out, there will be no reason to continue. When I hear from Vienna, I'll tell you the result. Quiet! I can hear my wife's voice.

[*Lady Chiltern comes in wearing a hat.*]

LADY CHILTERN: Good afternoon, Lord Goring!

LORD GORING: Good afternoon, Lady Chiltern! Have you been in the Park?

LADY CHILTERN: No, I have just come from a meeting at the Women's Club. Everyone was talking about you, Robert. You're very popular! I'll be back in a minute. I'm only going to take my hat off. [*She goes out.*]

SIR ROBERT [*taking Lord Goring's hand*]: You have been a good friend to me, Arthur, a very good friend.

LORD GORING: I haven't done anything for you. Not yet.

SIR ROBERT: I have talked to you honestly and you have listened. That's something. Why couldn't I do that before? And I would love to be honest now. [*He walks sadly towards the door.*] I'll see you again soon, Arthur, won't I?

LORD GORING: Yes, of course. Any time. I'm going to a party tonight, but I'll come to your house tomorrow night.

SIR ROBERT: Thank you.

[*As he reaches the door, Lady Chiltern returns.*]

LADY CHILTERN: Robert, you aren't going, are you?

SIR ROBERT: I have some letters to write, dear.

LADY CHILTERN [*going to him*]: You work too hard, Robert. You never think of yourself, and you are looking tired.

SIR ROBERT: It's nothing, dear, nothing. [*He kisses her and goes out.*]

Scene 2

LADY CHILTERN [*to Lord Goring*]: Sit down. I'm so glad you have come. I want to talk to you.

LORD GORING: You want to talk to me about Mrs Cheveley?

LADY CHILTERN: Yes. You have guessed it. Robert told me something after you left last night. We spoke about the Argentine Canal plan. He promised to help Mrs Cheveley. Of course Robert wrote to her immediately. He took back his promise.

LORD GORING: Yes, he told me.

LADY CHILTERN: Robert has always done the right thing. [*She looks at Lord Goring, but he stays silent.*] Don't you agree with me? You're our greatest friend, Lord Goring. You and I know Robert very well. He has no secrets from me. And I don't think he has any from you.

LORD GORING [*slowly*]: No, I don't think that he has any secrets from me.

LADY CHILTERN: Am I right in my opinion of him? Speak to me honestly. You have nothing to hide, have you?

LORD GORING: Nothing. But, my dear Lady Chiltern, when a man wants to be successful, he will do anything.

LADY CHILTERN: What do you mean?

LORD GORING: He will do anything. Of course I'm only talking about life in general.

LADY CHILTERN [*seriously*]: I hope so. Why are you looking at me so strangely, Lord Goring?

LORD GORING: Lady Chiltern, you have very strong opinions. Every man can be weak at some time. Even men like my father or Robert can make mistakes. I'll give you an example. Imagine that a man writes a letter to someone.

LADY CHILTERN: What kind of letter?

LORD GORING: A letter that must stay secret.

LADY CHILTERN: Robert can't do anything like that. It's impossible.

LORD GORING [*after a minute*]: Everyone can make a mistake. And everybody can do something that is wrong.

LADY CHILTERN: I'm surprised at you. Do you believe that all people are bad?

LORD GORING [*standing up*]: No, Lady Chiltern, I don't. And I believe that all people should be kind. If you are ever in trouble, Lady Chiltern, call me. I'll help you in every way that I can.

LADY CHILTERN [*looking at him in surprise*]: Lord Goring, I have never heard you talk seriously before.

LORD GORING [*laughing*]: You must excuse me, Lady Chiltern. It won't happen again.

LADY CHILTERN: But I like it when you are serious.

Scene 3

[*Mabel Chiltern comes in, wearing a beautiful dress.*]

MABEL CHILTERN: Dear Gertrude, please don't say that to Lord Goring! He's *never* serious. Good afternoon, Lord Goring! Please don't be serious!

LORD GORING: I'm sorry, Miss Mabel. I must. And I'm afraid that I must go now.

19

MABEL CHILTERN: Just when I have come in! You aren't very polite!

LORD GORING: No, I'm not.

MABEL CHILTERN: I would like to change you. Perhaps it's too late now.

LORD GORING [*smiling*]: I'm not sure.

MABEL CHILTERN: Will you ride with me tomorrow morning?

LORD GORING: Yes, at ten.

MABEL CHILTERN: Don't forget.

LORD GORING: Of course I won't. [*taking his hat*] Goodbye, Lady Chiltern! Please remember what I said.

LADY CHILTERN: I will. But I don't know why you said it.

LORD GORING: I don't know either. Goodbye, Miss Mabel!

MABEL CHILTERN: Why don't you stay? I would love to talk to you.

LORD GORING: I'll see you at ten tomorrow. [*He goes out.*]

MABEL CHILTERN: And I must go too. I'm going to Lady Basildon's. [*She kisses Lady Chiltern and goes out, then runs back in.*] Oh, Gertrude, do you know who is coming to see you? That terrible Mrs Cheveley, in a beautiful dress. Did you invite her?

LADY CHILTERN [*standing up*]: Mrs Cheveley! Coming to see me? Impossible!

MABEL CHILTERN: But it's true! She's arriving now.

LADY CHILTERN: You don't need to wait, Mabel. Remember, Lady Basildon is expecting you.

[*Mabel Chiltern leaves. Mason comes in.*]

Scene 4

MASON: Lady Markby. Mrs Cheveley.

[*Lady Markby and Mrs Cheveley come in. Mason leaves.*]

LADY CHILTERN [*going to meet them*]: Dear Lady Markby, how nice to see you. [*She shakes hands with her and looks at Mrs Cheveley.*] Won't you sit down, Mrs Cheveley?

MRS CHEVELEY: Thanks. [*They all sit down.*]

LADY MARKBY: Dear Gertrude, Mrs Cheveley has lost a gold brooch. Has anybody found it?

LADY CHILTERN: Here?

MRS CHEVELEY: Yes. I missed it when I got back to the hotel.

LADY CHILTERN: I haven't heard anything about it. But I'll ask Mason. [*She rings for him.*]

MRS CHEVELEY: Oh, don't worry, Lady Chiltern. I probably lost it before I came here.

[*Mason comes in.*]

LADY CHILTERN: Has anyone found a gold brooch this morning, Mason?

MASON: No, my lady.

MRS CHEVELEY: It really isn't important, Lady Chiltern. I'm sorry for the trouble.

LADY CHILTERN [*coldly*]: Oh, it's no trouble. Mason, you can bring tea.

[*Mason goes out.*]

LADY MARKBY: I'm afraid I can't stay for tea. I have promised to visit Lady Brancaster. She's in very great trouble. Her daughter is going to get married, but the man comes from a very ordinary family. It's really very sad. [*standing up*] Gertrude, can I leave Mrs Cheveley with you? I'll return in a quarter of an hour.

LADY CHILTERN [*standing up*]: Oh, I would like to have a few minutes' conversation with Mrs Cheveley.

MRS CHEVELEY: How very kind of you, Lady Chiltern!

LADY MARKBY: I'm sure you want to talk about your happy schooldays. Goodbye, dear Gertrude! [*She goes out. Lady Chiltern and Mrs Cheveley sit down. Mason comes in and puts the tea on a small table close to Lady Chiltern.*]

LADY CHILTERN: Shall I give you some tea, Mrs Cheveley?

MRS CHEVELEY: Thanks.

[*Mason hands Mrs Cheveley a cup of tea. He goes out.*]

MRS CHEVELEY: A wonderful woman, Lady Markby, isn't she? She talks a lot and says very little.

[*Lady Chiltern is silent. Then the eyes of the two women meet. Lady Chiltern looks serious. Mrs Cheveley has a little smile on her face.*]

LADY CHILTERN: Mrs Cheveley, I didn't invite you to my house last night. Lady Markby did. I didn't know your name. And I will *never* invite you to my house.

MRS CHEVELEY [*smiling brightly*]: Really? After all these years you haven't changed, Gertrude.

LADY CHILTERN: I never change.

MRS CHEVELEY [*looking surprised*]: Then life has taught you nothing?

LADY CHILTERN: Yes, it has taught me something. If people are dishonest once, they will be dishonest a second time. And honest people should keep away from them.

MRS CHEVELEY: Do you follow that rule for everyone?

LADY CHILTERN: Yes, for everyone.

MRS CHEVELEY: Then I'm very sorry for you, Gertrude.

LADY CHILTERN: So I can't see you again during your visit to London. Do you understand that now?

MRS CHEVELEY [*sitting back in her chair*]: Gertrude, I know you dislike me. And I have always hated you. But I have come here to help you.

LADY CHILTERN [*angrily*]: As you wanted to help my husband last night? But I saved him from that.

MRS CHEVELEY [*standing up quickly*]: It was you! You told him to write to me. You told him to break his promise!

LADY CHILTERN: Yes.

MRS CHEVELEY: Then you must tell him to keep it. He must give his answer tomorrow morning. He must help me with this great plan.

LADY CHILTERN: This *dishonest* plan.

MRS CHEVELEY: You can call it what you like. I have great power over your husband. You must tell him to help me.

LADY CHILTERN [*standing up and going towards her*]: You're a very rude woman. My husband will not talk to you.

MRS CHEVELEY [*coldly*]: In this world we often meet people who are the same as us. Your husband and I are dishonest. You and he are very different. But he and I are closer than friends. We are enemies who have made the same mistakes.

LADY CHILTERN: Don't say that my husband is like you! And don't tell us what to do! Leave my house!

[*Sir Robert comes in behind the two women. He hears his wife's last words and he sees Mrs Cheveley. He looks very nervous.*]

MRS CHEVELEY: *Your* house! This house was bought dishonestly. [*She turns round and sees Sir Robert.*] Ask him where his money came from! He sold a government secret to a businessman! Ask him about his success.

LADY CHILTERN: It's not true! Robert! It's not true!

MRS CHEVELEY [*pointing her finger at him*]: Look at him! Can he answer? No, he can't!

SIR ROBERT: Go immediately! You have done your worst.

MRS CHEVELEY: My worst? I haven't finished with you yet. You must do what I say before tomorrow at twelve o'clock. If you don't, I'll tell the world Robert Chiltern's secret.

[*Sir Robert rings. Mason comes in.*]

SIR ROBERT: Take Mrs Cheveley to the door.

[*Mrs Cheveley looks surprised. Then she looks very closely at Lady Chiltern. Lady Chiltern does not look at her. Sir Robert is standing*] *close to the door. Mrs Cheveley stops and looks him straight in the face. She then goes out. Mason follows her and closes the door. Lady Chiltern stands like someone in a terrible dream. Then she turns and looks at her husband.*]

Scene 5

LADY CHILTERN: You sold a government secret for money! You began your life dishonestly! You didn't earn your success! Oh, tell me it isn't true! Lie to me! Lie to me!

SIR ROBERT: It's quite true. But, Gertrude, listen to me. I can explain everything. [*He goes towards her.*]

LADY CHILTERN: Don't come near me. Don't touch me. I have never known you! You sold yourself for money. You're worse than a thief. You lied to everyone.

SIR ROBERT [*running towards her*]: Gertrude! Gertrude!

LADY CHILTERN [*pushing him back*]: No, don't speak! Your voice brings back terrible memories. I loved your words and I loved you. Now I hate those memories. I thought you were perfect. You were different from other men. You seemed so good and honest. Why did I give my life to you?

SIR ROBERT: That was your mistake. All women make that mistake. You all think that we are perfect. But all men make mistakes. Why don't you forgive us? We need your love *because* we aren't perfect. I was afraid to show myself to you. I was afraid to lose your love. But now I *have* lost it. And last night that woman offered to help me, but you stopped her. Now I'll lose everything! I have always loved you. But now you have taken away my future!

[*He leaves the room. Lady Chiltern stands for a minute, then sits down heavily in an armchair. She hides her face in her hands and cries like a child.*]

24

'You're worse than a thief.'

Act 3   A Stolen Letter

Scene 1

[*The library in Lord Goring's house. There are three doors — on the right, on the left and at the back. Phipps is putting some newspapers on a desk. Lord Goring comes in. He is wearing evening clothes and a hat. Phipps takes his coat and hat.*]

LORD GORING: Are there any letters, Phipps?

PHIPPS [*handing him the letters*]: Three, my lord.

LORD GORING [*taking them*]: I want my carriage in twenty minutes. That's all.

PHIPPS: Yes, my lord. [*He goes out.*]

LORD GORING [*to himself, holding up a letter in a pink envelope*]: Lady Chiltern's handwriting. That's strange. Why didn't Robert write to me? What does Lady Chiltern want to tell me? [*He sits at his desk, then opens and reads the letter.*] 'I want you. I trust you. I am coming to you. Gertrude.' So she has found out everything! Poor woman! [*He takes his watch from his pocket and looks at it.*] But what a time to visit! Ten o'clock! I won't be able to go to the Berkshires'. Well, she must stay with her husband and help him. I'll tell her that. She will be here soon. I must tell Phipps. [*He rings and Phipps comes in.*]

PHIPPS: Lord Caversham.

LORD GORING: Oh, why do parents always arrive at the wrong time? [*Lord Caversham comes in.*] I'm very pleased to see you, my dear father. [*He goes to meet him.*]

LORD CAVERSHAM: Take my coat off.

LORD GORING: Have you got enough time, Father?

LORD CAVERSHAM: Of course I have, sir. Which is the most comfortable chair?

LORD GORING: This one, Father. It's my own chair.

LORD CAVERSHAM: Thank you. [*sitting down*] I want to have a serious conversation with you, sir.

LORD GORING: My dear father! At this time?

LORD CAVERSHAM: Well, sir, it's ten o'clock. What's wrong with that? I think it's an excellent time!

LORD GORING: Well, Father, this isn't the right time for *me*. I'm very sorry. My doctor says I must not have any serious conversation after ten. If I do, I talk in my sleep.

LORD CAVERSHAM: Talk in your sleep, sir? That doesn't matter. You aren't married.

LORD GORING: No, Father, I'm not married.

LORD CAVERSHAM: I have come to talk to you about that, sir. You have got to get married immediately. I was married when I was your age. You can't just live for fun. Every important man is married now. Look at Robert Chiltern. He has a good position. How did he get there? Hard work, honesty and marriage with a good woman. Why don't you do the same thing?

LORD GORING: I think I will, Father.

LORD CAVERSHAM: I hope so, sir. Then I will be happy. Your mother and I are quite unhappy. And you are the reason. You are heartless, sir, quite heartless.

LORD GORING: I hope not, Father.

LORD CAVERSHAM: Now is the time for you to get married. You are thirty-four years of age, sir.

LORD GORING: Yes, Father, but I only look thirty-two. I'll come and see you tomorrow. We can talk about anything you like. I'll help you with your coat.

LORD CAVERSHAM: No, sir; I have come here this evening for a reason. Put down my coat, sir.

LORD GORING: Yes, Father. But let's go into another room. [*He rings for a servant.*] It's too cold here.

[*Phipps comes in.*]

27

LORD GORING: Phipps, is there a good fire in the smoking room?

PHIPPS: Yes, my lord.

LORD GORING: Go in there, Father. You will be much warmer. [*Lord Caversham goes out.*] Phipps, a lady is coming to see me on business this evening. Take her into the other sitting room when she arrives.

PHIPPS: Yes, my lord.

LORD GORING: Do not bring in any other visitors. Not for any reason. It's very important

PHIPPS: I understand, my lord.

[*Someone rings at the door.*]

LORD GORING: Ah! That's probably the lady. I'll see her now.

[*Just as he is going towards the door, Lord Caversham comes in again.*]

LORD CAVERSHAM: Well, sir? Must I wait for you?

LORD GORING [*worried*]: In a minute, Father. Please excuse me. [*Lord Caversham goes out.*] Remember, Phipps – into that room.

PHIPPS: Yes, my lord. [*He and Lord Goring go out.*]

Scene 2

[*Phipps comes in with Mrs Cheveley. She is wearing a green and silver dress and a long black coat.*]

MRS CHEVELEY: Is Lord Goring here?

PHIPPS: Lord Goring is busy with Lord Caversham, madam.

MRS CHEVELEY [*to herself*]: What a good son!

PHIPPS: Lord Goring will see you in the sitting room, madam. He would like you to wait there, if you don't mind.

MRS CHEVELEY [*with a look of surprise*]: Lord Goring is expecting me?

PHIPPS: Yes, madam. Lord Goring said, 'If a lady comes, ask her to wait in the sitting room.' Lord Goring spoke very clearly. [*He goes into the sitting room and turns on the lights.*]

MRS CHEVELEY [*to herself*]: How thoughtful of him! [*She goes towards the sitting room and looks in.*] Oh! How boring! Unmarried men never have nice sitting rooms. I'll have to change all this. [*She goes over to the desk and picks up some letters.*] Bills and cards. But who writes to him on pink paper? How silly! It's too romantic! [*She picks up the letter.*] I know that handwriting. That is Gertrude Chiltern's. I remember it perfectly. But why is Gertrude writing to him? She's probably saying terrible things about me. [*She reads it.*] 'I trust you. I want you. I am coming to you. Gertrude.' [*A pleased look comes over her face. She is going to steal the letter, but Phipps returns.*]

PHIPPS: The sitting room is ready, madam.

MRS CHEVELEY: Thank you.

[*She quickly hides the letter under a large book. She goes into the sitting room. Phipps closes the door and leaves. Then the door slowly opens, and Mrs Cheveley comes out. She walks quietly towards the desk. Suddenly we can hear voices. Mrs Cheveley looks nervous and returns unhappily to the sitting room. Lord Goring and Lord Caversham come in.*]

Scene 3

LORD GORING [*excitedly*]: So, my dear father, you want me to get married. But I want to choose the time and the place. And the person! That's the most important thing!

LORD CAVERSHAM [*impatiently*]: That's *my* business, sir. I'm sure that you will not choose well. Your feelings aren't important now. Our land and our money are more important. Feelings are important later in married life.

LORD GORING: Yes. Feelings are important when married people aren't happy together, Father. Don't you agree? [*He helps Lord Caversham put on his coat.*]

LORD CAVERSHAM: Yes, of course. I mean, of course not. You aren't talking sensibly tonight. When you get married, you must be sensible.

LORD GORING: Yes, Father. [*He and Lord Caversham go out.*]

Scene 4

[*Lord Goring comes in unhappily with Sir Robert.*]

SIR ROBERT: My dear Arthur, what good luck! I'm pleased to see you. Do you know what your servant told me? 'Lord Goring is not at home.'

LORD GORING: In fact, I'm terribly busy tonight, Robert. I don't want to see anyone. I was even cold to my father.

SIR ROBERT: Ah! But you *must* see me, Arthur. You're my best friend. Perhaps you will be my *only* friend tomorrow. My wife has discovered everything.

LORD GORING: Ah! I guessed that!

SIR ROBERT [*looking at him*]: Really! How?

LORD GORING [*after a short silence*]: Oh, it was the look on your face. Who told her?

SIR ROBERT: Mrs Cheveley. Now my wife knows my secret. Lord Radley trusted me with a secret. Then I sold it like an ordinary thief. Lord Radley never found out before he died. Oh, why didn't *I* die? [*He hides his face in his hands.*]

LORD GORING [*after a silence*]: Have you heard anything from Vienna?

SIR ROBERT [*looking up*]: Yes, I got a reply tonight. They don't have much information about her. She has quite a high position in society. Baron Arnheim left her most of his money. That's all I know.

LORD GORING: So she isn't a spy, then?

SIR ROBERT: Spies are finished. The newspapers do their work now.

LORD GORING: And they do it terribly well.

SIR ROBERT: I don't know what to do, Arthur. You're my only friend. I can trust you completely, can't I?

LORD GORING: My dear Robert, of course. [*He rings.*] Will you excuse me for a minute, Robert? I have to talk to my servant.

SIR ROBERT: Of course.

[*Phipps comes in. He and Lord Goring go to a corner of the room and talk quietly.*]

LORD GORING: Phipps, that lady will be here soon. Tell her that I'm out. Say that I have suddenly left London. Do you understand?

PHIPPS: The lady is in that room, my lord. You told me to take her there, my lord.

LORD GORING: You did the right thing. [*Phipps goes out. Lord Goring talks to himself.*] This is terrible! No, it will be all right. I'll talk to her through the door.

SIR ROBERT: Arthur, what should I do? I feel lost. I'm like a ship without a sail. I'm travelling at night without a star.

LORD GORING: Robert, you love your wife, don't you?

SIR ROBERT: I love her more than anything in the world. I thought that success was everything. It is not. Love is the greatest thing in the world. But she doesn't love me now.

LORD GORING: Has she never made a mistake in her life? If she has, she will forgive you.

SIR ROBERT: My wife! Never! She does not understand mistakes or weakness. I'm as weak as other men. She's as cold and perfect as all good women. She will never forgive me. But I love her, Arthur.

LORD GORING: Your wife *will* forgive you. Perhaps she is forgiving you right now. She loves you, Robert. Why won't she forgive you?

SIR ROBERT: She must! She must! [*He hides his face in his hands.*] But I have to tell you something, Arthur. I have decided what to do tonight in the House. They will discuss the Argentine Canal at eleven. [*A chair falls in the sitting room.*] What's that?

LORD GORING: Nothing.

SIR ROBERT: I heard a chair fall in the next room. Someone is listening.

LORD GORING: No, no. There is nobody there.

SIR ROBERT: There *is* someone. There are lights in the room, and the door is open. Someone has heard every secret of my life. Arthur, what does this mean?

LORD GORING: Robert, sit down. You are excited and nervous. There is nobody in that room.

SIR ROBERT: Are you sure? I want to look in that room. I want to know that my secrets are safe.

LORD GORING: No! Robert, this must stop. I have already told you. There is nobody in that room. That's enough.

SIR ROBERT [*running to the door of the room*]: It is *not* enough. I must go into this room. How can you refuse me?

LORD GORING: Don't do it! There *is* someone there. Someone who you must not see.

SIR ROBERT: Ah, I thought so! [*He goes into the room.*]

LORD GORING: Oh, no! His own wife!

[*Sir Robert comes back, looking very angry.*]

SIR ROBERT: How can you explain that? What is that woman doing here?

LORD GORING: Robert, that lady has never hurt you. I promise you that. She came here for you. She wants to save you. She's honest and true. She loves only you.

SIR ROBERT: How can you say that? What are you planning together? You're not trying to help me. I trusted you but you are my enemy.

LORD GORING: It isn't true, Robert. Ask her to come out. I will explain. I promise you.

SIR ROBERT: I am leaving, sir. You have lied enough. [*He goes out.*]

Scene 5

[*Lord Goring runs to the door of the sitting room. Mrs Cheveley comes out, looking very amused.*]

MRS CHEVELEY [*very politely*]: Good evening, Lord Goring!

LORD GORING: Mrs Cheveley! Oh, no! What were you doing in my sitting room?

MRS CHEVELEY: Just listening at the door. I love listening at doors. I always hear so many wonderful things.

LORD GORING: Isn't that dangerous?

MRS CHEVELEY: Oh! Yes, of course. [*She makes a sign to him to take her coat off. He does.*]

LORD GORING: You want to sell me Robert Chiltern's letter, don't you?

MRS CHEVELEY: How did you guess that?

LORD GORING: Because you haven't said anything about it. Have you got it with you?

MRS CHEVELEY [*sitting down*]: Oh, no! A well-made dress has no pockets.

LORD GORING: What is your price for it?

MRS CHEVELEY: You sound very English when you say that. The English think that money can solve every problem. My dear Arthur, I have much more money than you. And I have as much as Robert Chiltern. I don't want money.

LORD GORING: What do you want then, Mrs Cheveley?

MRS CHEVELEY: Why don't you call me Laura?

LORD GORING: I don't like the name.

MRS CHEVELEY: You loved it before.

LORD GORING: Yes, that's why.

[*Mrs Cheveley invites him to sit down next to her. He smiles and sits down.*]

MRS CHEVELEY: Arthur, you loved me before.

LORD GORING: Yes.

MRS CHEVELEY: And you asked me to be your wife.

LORD GORING: Because I loved you.

MRS CHEVELEY: And you left me because of poor old Lord Mortlake. He tried to kiss me in the garden. Do you remember that?

LORD GORING: Yes. And you were paid for the broken promise. I remember that too.

MRS CHEVELEY: At that time I was poor and you were rich.

LORD GORING: Yes. That's why you loved me.

MRS CHEVELEY: But I really *did* love you, Arthur.

LORD GORING: My dear Mrs Cheveley, you have never known anything about love. You are much too clever.

MRS CHEVELEY [*after a silence*]: I am tired of living abroad. I want to come back to London. I want to have a charming house here. And I'm feeling romantic. You are the only person I have ever loved. I knew that when I saw you last night at the Chilterns'. So I'll give you Robert Chiltern's letter if you promise to marry me.

LORD GORING: Are you serious? I'll be a very bad husband.

MRS CHEVELEY: I don't mind bad husbands. I have had two. They amused me very well.

LORD GORING: You mean that you amused *yourself* very well.

MRS CHEVELEY: What do you know about my married life?

LORD GORING: Nothing, but I can read it like a book.

MRS CHEVELEY: What kind of book?

LORD GORING [*standing up*]: A bank book.

MRS CHEVELEY: You're very rude! So you refuse to marry me. And you refuse to help your best friend, Robert Chiltern.

LORD GORING: He made a mistake when he was young. I know that it was dishonest. But he isn't really like that.

MRS CHEVELEY: You men always defend other men!

LORD GORING: And you women always fight other women!

MRS CHEVELEY [*angrily*]: I only fight one woman – Gertrude Chiltern. I hate her. I hate her now more than ever.

LORD GORING: Why? You have made her life very difficult.

MRS CHEVELEY [*coldly*]: Gertrude Chiltern doesn't know anything about life. That's why we were never friends. Well, Arthur, our romantic conversation is finished. And it *was* romantic, wasn't it? I wanted to marry you. And I offered you Robert Chiltern's letter. But you refused. So Sir Robert must tell the House about the great Argentine Canal plan or I'll tell his secret.

LORD GORING: You mustn't do that. That's terrible.

MRS CHEVELEY: No, that's business. And you can't mix feelings with business. I offered to sell the letter to Robert Chiltern. Now he can pay me my price or pay a greater price. That's all. I must go. Goodbye. Won't you shake hands?

LORD GORING: With you? No. You have done a terrible thing. You talked about love, but you don't understand it. You went to a good, honest woman's house this afternoon. She loved her husband very much. But you tried to kill that love. You tried to destroy her life. I can't forgive you for that.

MRS CHEVELEY: Arthur, you are unfair to me. I didn't go there for that reason. I lost a brooch last night, perhaps at the Chilterns' house. I was only looking for my brooch.

LORD GORING: A gold brooch?

MRS CHEVELEY: Yes. How do you know?

LORD GORING: Because I found it. I forgot to tell the servants about it. [*He goes over to the desk and opens it.*] This is the brooch, isn't it? [*He holds up the brooch.*]

MRS CHEVELEY: Yes. I'm so glad to see it. It was . . . a present.

LORD GORING: Won't you wear it?

MRS CHEVELEY: Yes, if you put it on. [*Lord Goring suddenly puts it on her wrist.*] Can I wear it as a bracelet? I didn't know that.

LORD GORING: Really?

MRS CHEVELEY [*holding out her arm*]: No, but it looks very nice on me as a bracelet, doesn't it?

LORD GORING: Yes. I haven't seen it for a long time.

MRS CHEVELEY: Have you seen it before? When?

LORD GORING [*calmly*]: Ten years ago, on Lady Berkshire.

MRS CHEVELEY [*surprised*]: What do you mean?

LORD GORING: You stole that bracelet from my cousin, Mary Berkshire. I gave it to her when she got married. A poor servant lost her job when it disappeared. Then I saw it again last night. I didn't say anything. But I have found the thief.

MRS CHEVELEY [*angrily*]: It isn't true.

LORD GORING: You know it's true. You look like a thief.

MRS CHEVELEY: It isn't true. I have never seen this bracelet before. I'll tell everyone that. [*She tries to take the bracelet off her arm, but she fails. Lord Goring watches and looks amused.*]

LORD GORING: There's one problem when you steal something, Mrs Cheveley. You don't know how it works. You can't take that bracelet off. It's quite difficult, isn't it?

MRS CHEVELEY: You animal! That isn't fair! [*She tries again to take the bracelet off, but she fails. She becomes angrier. She stops and looks at Lord Goring.*] What are you going to do?

LORD GORING: I'm going to ring for my servant. He will get the police.

MRS CHEVELEY [*afraid*]: The police? Why?

LORD GORING: You have broken the law. That's why we have police.

[*Mrs Cheveley now looks very afraid. Her face looks old and ugly.*]

'I have never seen this bracelet before. I'll tell everyone that.'

MRS CHEVELEY: Don't do that. I'll do anything you want. Anything in the world you want.

LORD GORING: Give me Robert Chiltern's letter.

MRS CHEVELEY: I haven't got it with me. I'll give it to you tomorrow.

LORD GORING: You know you are lying. Give it to me immediately.

[*Mrs Cheveley pulls the letter out, and hands it to him. She looks terribly unhappy. Lord Goring takes the letter and looks at it. Then he burns it and he takes the bracelet off Mrs Cheveley's arm.*]

LORD GORING: You are very sensible, Mrs Cheveley.

MRS CHEVELEY [*looking at a corner of Lady Chiltern's letter, on the desk, under the book*]: Please get me a glass of water.

LORD GORING: Of course. [*He goes and pours a glass of water. While his back is turned, Mrs Cheveley steals the letter. When Lord Goring returns, she refuses the water.*]

MRS CHEVELEY: Thank you. Will you help me put on my coat?

LORD GORING: Gladly. [*He helps her.*]

MRS CHEVELEY: Thanks. I'll never try to hurt Robert Chiltern again.

LORD GORING: You will not be able to, Mrs Cheveley.

MRS CHEVELEY: Well, even if I can, I won't. In fact, I'm going to help him.

LORD GORING: I'm pleased to hear it. You have changed completely.

MRS CHEVELEY: Yes. I feel sorry for him. He's an honest man. But his wife is so dishonest. What a pity.

LORD GORING: What are you talking about?

MRS CHEVELEY: I have Gertrude Chiltern's secret in my pocket.

LORD GORING: What do you mean?

MRS CHEVELEY [*angrily*]: I mean her love letter. The one that she wrote to you tonight. I'm going to send it to Robert Chiltern.

LORD GORING: Love letter?

MRS CHEVELEY [*laughing*]: 'I want you. I trust you. I am coming to you. Gertrude.'

[*Lord Goring runs to the desk and finds the empty envelope. He turns round.*]

LORD GORING: You thief! Why are you always stealing? Give me back that letter. I'll take it from you. You will not leave my room until I have it. [*He runs towards her. Mrs Cheveley immediately rings for Phipps and he comes in.*]

MRS CHEVELEY [*after a silence*]: Lord Goring rang. You can take me to the door. Good night, Lord Goring!

[*She goes out followed by Phipps. Her face looks young and happy. She looks closely at Lord Goring as she leaves.*]

Act 4   New Lives

Scene 1

[*In the sitting room at Sir Robert's house. Lord Goring is standing with his hands in his pockets. He is looking quite bored. He takes out his watch and looks at it. Then he rings for the servant.*]

LORD GORING [*to himself*]: This is terrible. There's nobody in this house. I want to talk to somebody. And I'm full of interesting information. I feel like the latest newspaper.

[*James comes in.*]

JAMES: Sir Robert is still at the Foreign Office, my lord.
LORD GORING: Hasn't Lady Chiltern come down?
JAMES: Lady Chiltern has not yet left her room. Miss Chiltern has just come in from riding.
LORD GORING [*to himself*]: Ah! Good!

JAMES: Lord Caversham is waiting for Sir Robert in the library. He knows that you are here.

LORD GORING: Thank you! Now please tell him that I have gone.

JAMES [*politely*]: Yes, my lord. [*He goes out.*]

LORD GORING: Really, I don't want to meet my father every day. It's much too exciting. [*He sits down and reads a newspaper. Lord Caversham comes in.*]

LORD CAVERSHAM: Well, sir, what are you doing here? Nothing? That's how you usually spend your time.

LORD GORING [*throwing down the paper and standing up*]: No, my dear father, I *am* doing something. I have come to visit.

LORD CAVERSHAM: Do you remember what I said last night? Have you been thinking about it?

LORD GORING: Yes, Father. Only that.

LORD CAVERSHAM: Are you ready to get married yet?

LORD GORING [*happily*]: Not yet. But I hope to be ready before lunchtime.

LORD CAVERSHAM: I never know when you are serious.

LORD GORING: I don't either, Father. [*They are silent.*]

LORD CAVERSHAM: You *have* read *The Times* this morning, haven't you?

LORD GORING [*uninterestedly*]: *The Times*? Of course not. I only read *The Morning Post*. It's all about London Society.

LORD CAVERSHAM: So you haven't read *The Times*? It's all about Robert Chiltern.

LORD GORING [*surprised*]: No! What does it say?

LORD CAVERSHAM: What do you think, sir? Good things, of course. He made a fine speech in the House last night. It was about this Argentine Canal plan.

LORD GORING: Ah. And was . . . was Chiltern for or against the plan?

LORD CAVERSHAM: For it or against it, sir? You don't know him very well! He spoke very strongly against it. This is his most important speech. You should read *The Times*, sir. [*He opens* The Times *newspaper and reads.*] 'Sir Robert Chiltern ... well-known in political life ... excellent speaker ... honest ... high ideals ... important position in English government ...' They will never say that about *you*, sir. Why don't you do something useful in life?

LORD GORING: I'm still too young.

LORD CAVERSHAM [*impatiently*]: I hate that excuse, sir. Too many people say that. Why don't you ask Miss Chiltern to marry you? She's very pretty. Do you think she will accept you?

LORD GORING: I don't know.

[*Mabel Chiltern comes in.*]

MABEL CHILTERN: Oh! ... How do you do, Lord Caversham? I hope Lady Caversham is quite well.

LORD CAVERSHAM: Lady Caversham is the same, the same.

LORD GORING: Good morning, Miss Mabel!

MABEL CHILTERN [*not looking at Lord Goring and speaking to Lord Caversham*]: And how about Lady Caversham's hats? Are *they* better?

LORD CAVERSHAM: No, I'm afraid that they are much worse.

LORD GORING: Good morning, Miss Mabel!

MABEL CHILTERN [*to Lord Caversham*]: Perhaps they should see a doctor.

LORD CAVERSHAM [*smiling at her*]: Lady Caversham will not like that. She's the only one who can touch them.

LORD GORING [*more loudly*]: Good morning, Miss Mabel!

MABEL CHILTERN [*turning round in surprise*]: Oh, are you here? You didn't come riding with me in the Park. So I'm never going to speak to you again.

LORD GORING: Oh, please don't say that. I love it when you listen to me. You're the best listener in London.

MABEL CHILTERN: Lord Goring, I never believe anything that you say.

LORD CAVERSHAM: You are quite right, my dear.

MABEL CHILTERN [to Lord Caversham]: Do you think you can change your son? Can you tell him to be good sometimes?

LORD CAVERSHAM: I'm sorry, Miss Chiltern. My son never listens to me. He's very heartless, very heartless. Now, my dear, I must say goodbye.

MABEL CHILTERN: Oh! You're not going to leave me alone with Lord Goring? It's too early in the morning.

LORD CAVERSHAM: I'm sorry. I can't take him with me to Downing Street.* The Prime Minister isn't meeting unemployed people today. [He shakes hands with Mabel Chiltern. Then he puts on his hat. As he goes out, he looks angrily at Lord Goring.]

Scene 2

MABEL CHILTERN: I don't like people who break promises.

LORD GORING: They are terrible.

MABEL CHILTERN: I'm glad that you agree. But don't look so pleased about it.

LORD GORING: I can't help it. I always look pleased when I'm with you.

MABEL CHILTERN [sadly]: Do I have to stay with you, then?

LORD GORING: Of course.

MABEL CHILTERN: Well, if I have to stay, I won't. So I'm afraid that I must leave you.

LORD GORING: Please don't, Miss Mabel. I have something very special to say to you.

MABEL CHILTERN [very excitedly]: Oh! Are you going to ask me to marry you?

LORD GORING [surprised]: Well, yes, I am.

MABEL CHILTERN [pleased]: I'm so glad.

*Downing Street: the London address of the Prime Minister's home and office

LORD GORING: I love you.

MABEL CHILTERN: I know. Why haven't you said that before? I was expecting it.

LORD GORING: Mabel, please be serious. [*taking her hand*] I love you. Can't you love me a little in return?

MABEL CHILTERN: You silly Arthur! Don't you know that I love you? Everyone in London knows it except you. For the last six months I have told everyone.

[*Lord Goring takes her in his arms and kisses her. There is a happy silence.*]

LORD GORING: Of course you are too good for me, Mabel.

MABEL CHILTERN [*sitting close to him*]: Yes, dear, I know.

LORD GORING [*after a silence*]: And I'm . . . I'm a little over thirty.

MABEL CHILTERN: Dear, you look weeks younger than that.

LORD GORING [*happily*]: How sweet of you to say that! And I'm afraid that I spend a lot of money.

MABEL CHILTERN: But I do too, Arthur. So we will always agree. And now I must go and see Gertrude.

LORD GORING: Must you really? [*He kisses her.*]

MABEL CHILTERN: Yes.

LORD GORING: Then tell her that I want to talk to her. I have waited here all morning for her or Robert.

[*Lady Chiltern comes in.*]

LADY CHILTERN [*to Mabel*]: Good morning, dear! How pretty you are looking!

MABEL CHILTERN: How pale you are looking, Gertrude! You look lovely!

LADY CHILTERN: Good morning, Lord Goring!

LORD GORING [*politely*]: Good morning, Lady Chiltern!

MABEL CHILTERN [*quietly, to Lord Goring*]: I'll be in the garden room. Meet me under the second palm tree on the left.

LORD GORING: Second on the left?

MABEL CHILTERN [*with a look of surprise*]: Yes, the usual palm tree. [*She smiles and goes out.*]

Scene 3

LORD GORING: Lady Chiltern, I have some very good news. Mrs Cheveley gave me Robert's letter last night. I burned it. Robert is safe now.

LADY CHILTERN [*sitting on the sofa*]: Safe! Oh! I'm so glad. What a good friend you are to him – to us!

LORD GORING: Only one person is in danger now.

LADY CHILTERN: Who is that?

LORD GORING [*sitting down next to her*]: You.

LADY CHILTERN: Me? In danger? What do you mean?

LORD GORING: The word danger is too strong. But I have some bad news. Yesterday evening you wrote me a very beautiful letter. I am one of your oldest friends. And I am one of your husband's best friends. You asked for my help. Mrs Cheveley stole that letter from me.

LADY CHILTERN: Well, what can she do with it?

LORD GORING [*standing up*]: Lady Chiltern, I'll be quite honest with you. Mrs Cheveley is going to send it to your husband.

LADY CHILTERN: But why? I wanted to see you. I needed your help. What a terrible woman! Tell me what happened.

LORD GORING: Mrs Cheveley was hiding in the room next to my library. I didn't know. I thought that *you* were there. Robert came in when I wasn't expecting him. A chair fell in the room and he discovered her. He was very angry. He left and Mrs Cheveley stole your letter.

LADY CHILTERN: At what time did this happen?

LORD GORING: At half past ten. I have a suggestion. Let's tell Robert everything immediately.

LADY CHILTERN [*very surprised and worried*]: But you weren't expecting Mrs Cheveley! You were expecting *me* at half past ten at night! Do you want to tell him that?

LORD GORING: I think that he should know.

LADY CHILTERN [*standing up*]: Oh, I can't tell him! I can't!

LORD GORING [*seriously*]: You're wrong, Lady Chiltern.

LADY CHILTERN: No. He must not receive that letter. But his secretaries open his letters. What can we do?

LORD GORING: Please be calm, Lady Chiltern. I'll go and see his secretary. I'll ask him for the letter. [*He goes to the door and opens it.*] Oh! Robert is coming with the letter in his hand. It has reached him already.

LADY CHILTERN [*with a cry of pain*]: Oh! You have saved his life! What have you done with mine?

Scene 4

[*Sir Robert comes in. He is reading the letter. He comes towards his wife. He does not notice Lord Goring.*]

SIR ROBERT: 'I want you. I trust you. I am coming to you. Gertrude' Oh, my love! Is this true? Do you want me, Gertrude? [*Lord Goring makes a sign to Lady Chiltern. He asks her to accept her husband's mistake.*]

LADY CHILTERN: Yes.

SIR ROBERT: Do you trust me, Gertrude?

LADY CHILTERN: Yes.

SIR ROBERT: Ah! And do you love me too? Why didn't you write that?

LADY CHILTERN [*taking his hand*]: Because I loved you. [*Lord Goring goes out.*]

SIR ROBERT [*kissing his wife*]: Gertrude, you don't know what I feel. When I read your letter my fears left me. You still love me. Nothing matters except that.

LADY CHILTERN: You don't have to be afraid now. Mrs Cheveley has given the letter to Lord Goring. He has destroyed it.

SIR ROBERT: Are you sure of this, Gertrude?

LADY CHILTERN: Yes. Lord Goring has just told me.

SIR ROBERT: Then I'm safe! Oh! How wonderful! For two days I have been afraid. How did Arthur destroy my letter?

LADY CHILTERN: He burned it.

SIR ROBERT: Many well-known men would like to burn their mistakes. Is Arthur still here?

LADY CHILTERN: Yes, he's in the garden room.

SIR ROBERT: When I made that speech in the House I was afraid. But now I'm glad that I did.

LADY CHILTERN: And you are famous now.

SIR ROBERT: Yes, but I'm afraid of that too. I'm safe now, but Gertrude … should I leave the government? What do you think? [*He looks worriedly at his wife.*]

LADY CHILTERN [*happily*]: Oh yes, Robert, you should do that. You must.

SIR ROBERT: I'll lose a lot if I do that.

LADY CHILTERN: No. Life will be better.

[*Sir Robert walks up and down the room with a worried look. Then he puts his hand on his wife's shoulder.*]

SIR ROBERT: Would you like to live alone with me? We can live in the country away from London Society.

LADY CHILTERN: Oh, yes, Robert!

SIR ROBERT [*sadly*]: And your ambition for me? You always wanted me to succeed.

LADY CHILTERN: Oh, my ambition! I have none now. I only want to love you. Your ambition is the reason for your problems. Let's not talk about ambition.

[*Lord Goring returns, looking very happy.*]

SIR ROBERT [*going towards him*]: Arthur, thank you for helping me. How can I thank you? [*They shake hands.*]

LORD GORING: My dear friend, I'll tell you. Right now, under the usual palm tree ... I mean in the garden room ...

[*Mason comes in.*]

MASON: Lord Caversham.

LORD GORING: My dear father always arrives at the wrong time. He's very heartless, really very heartless.

Scene 5

[*Lord Caversham comes in and Mason goes out.*]

LORD CAVERSHAM: Good morning, Lady Chiltern! Chiltern, your speech was excellent! I have just left the Prime Minister. He has a very important government position for you.

SIR ROBERT [*with a look of happiness*]: Is that true?

LORD CAVERSHAM: Yes. Here is the Prime Minister's letter.

[*Sir Robert takes the letter from him and reads it.*]

SIR ROBERT: The position is in the Prime Minister's office!

LORD CAVERSHAM: Yes. We need you in political life today. You are honest and you always do the right thing.

[*Sir Robert is ready to accept the Prime Minister's offer. Then he sees his wife looking at him.*]

SIR ROBERT: I cannot accept this offer, Lord Caversham.

LORD CAVERSHAM: What do you mean, sir!

SIR ROBERT: I am going to leave the government.

LORD CAVERSHAM [*angrily*]: You're going to refuse the Prime Minister's offer? You're going to leave the government? I have never heard a more stupid idea. I'm sorry, Lady Chiltern. Chiltern, I'm sorry. [*to Lord Goring*] Don't smile like that, sir.

47

LORD GORING: No, Father.

LORD CAVERSHAM: Lady Chiltern, you are a sensible woman. Your husband is going to make a terrible mistake. Won't you stop him?

LADY CHILTERN: I think that my husband is right.

LORD CAVERSHAM [*surprised*]: Do you?

LADY CHILTERN [*taking her husband's hand*]: I love him for it. He is finer than I thought. [*to Sir Robert*] You will write to the Prime Minister now, won't you?

SIR ROBERT [*a little sadly*]: Yes, I must do it immediately. Please excuse me, Lord Caversham.

LADY CHILTERN: I can come with you, Robert, can't I?

SIR ROBERT: Yes, Gertrude. [*He and Lady Chiltern go out.*]

LORD GORING [*taking his father's arm*]: Oh! Just go in here for a minute, Father. The second palm tree on the left, the usual palm tree.

LORD CAVERSHAM: What, sir?

LORD GORING: I'm sorry, Father, I forgot. There is someone in the garden room. Please talk to her.

LORD CAVERSHAM: What about, sir?

LORD GORING: About me, Father.

LORD CAVERSHAM [*angrily*]: I can't say very much about that.

LORD GORING: No, Father, but the lady is like me. She likes people who don't say very much.

[*Lord Caversham goes out.*]

Scene 6

[*Lady Chiltern comes in.*]

LORD GORING: Lady Chiltern, why are you acting like Mrs Cheveley?

LADY CHILTERN [*surprised*]: I don't understand you.

48

LORD GORING: Mrs Cheveley tried to destroy your husband. She wanted him to be dishonest. You saved him from that. She wanted him to leave the government. She failed. But now you want the same thing.

LADY CHILTERN: Lord Goring?

LORD GORING [*very seriously*]: Lady Chiltern, please listen. You wrote me a letter last night. You trusted me. You wanted my help. Now you *really* need my help. You love Robert. He has become very successful. How can you take that away from him? What kind of life will he have? Women should not judge us. They should forgive us. Lady Chiltern, don't make this terrible mistake. Just love your husband and he will love you.

LADY CHILTERN: But my husband wants to leave the government. He suggested it first.

LORD GORING: He's doing it for you. He will give up anything for your love. But he's giving up too much. Please don't ask him to do this. Robert isn't perfect, but he is not a bad man either. If you take away his power, he will lose everything. He will even lose his power to feel love. Your husband's life is in your hands. Do not destroy it.

Scene 7

[*Sir Robert comes in.*]

SIR ROBERT: Gertrude, here is my letter. Shall I read it to you?

LADY CHILTERN: Show it to me.

[*Sir Robert hands her the letter. She reads it and then destroys it.*]

SIR ROBERT: What are you doing?

LADY CHILTERN: Men need success in their lives. Feelings are more important in women's lives. I have just learnt this from Lord Goring. And I will not destroy your life.

SIR ROBERT: Gertrude! Gertrude!

LADY CHILTERN: You can forget. Men easily forget. And I can forgive. That is how women help the world. I understand that now.

SIR ROBERT [*holding her in his arms*]: My wife! My wife! [*to Lord Goring*] Arthur, you have helped me so much. You wanted to ask me something when Lord Caversham came in.

LORD GORING: Robert, you are Mabel's brother. Will you give me permission to marry her?

LADY CHILTERN: Oh, I'm so glad! I'm so glad! [*She shakes hands with Lord Goring.*]

LORD GORING: Thank you, Lady Chiltern.

SIR ROBERT [*worried*]: You want my sister to be your wife?

LORD GORING: Yes.

SIR ROBERT: Arthur, I'm very sorry, but it's impossible. I have to think of Mabel's future. She will never be happy with you. I cannot give my permission.

LORD GORING: But I don't understand. Why not?

SIR ROBERT: Marriages without love are terrible. But it's worse when a marriage has love and trust only on one side. Then one heart will surely break.

LORD GORING: But I love Mabel. She's the only woman in my life.

LADY CHILTERN: Robert, they are in love. Why can't they be married?

SIR ROBERT: Arthur cannot give enough love to Mabel.

LORD GORING: Why are you saying that?

SIR ROBERT [*after a silence*]: Do you really want me to tell you?

LORD GORING: Of course I do.

SIR ROBERT: All right. Late yesterday evening I found Mrs Cheveley in your sitting room. I know you wanted to marry her in the past. She seems to have some power over you again. Last night you called her honest and true. Perhaps you are right. But I cannot give my sister's life into your hands. I want her to be happy.

LORD GORING: I have nothing more to say.

LADY CHILTERN: Robert, Lord Goring was not expecting Mrs Cheveley last night.

SIR ROBERT: Not Mrs Cheveley! Who, then?

LORD GORING: Lady Chiltern!

LADY CHILTERN: It was your own wife. Robert, yesterday afternoon Lord Goring offered to help me. He's our oldest and best friend. Then you told me your terrible secret. After that, I wrote to him. This is what I said. I trusted him. I needed him. I wanted to see him. [*Sir Robert takes the letter out of his pocket.*] Yes, that letter. But I didn't go to Lord Goring's. I was too proud. Mrs Cheveley went there and stole my letter. She sent it to you this morning. She wanted you to think . . . Oh! Robert, I can't talk about it!

SIR ROBERT: What! I trust you completely, Gertrude. I know that you are honest and good. Arthur, you can go to Mabel, and you have my best wishes!

LORD GORING: Well, I hope she hasn't changed her mind. I haven't seen her for nearly twenty minutes.

Scene 8

[*Mabel Chiltern and Lord Caversham come in.*]

MABEL CHILTERN: Lord Goring, your father's conversation is much better than yours. I'm only going to talk to Lord Caversham in the future. And always under the usual palm tree.

LORD GORING: My love! [*He kisses her.*]

LORD CAVERSHAM [*very surprised*]: What does this mean, sir? Has this charming, clever young lady accepted you? It can't be true!

LORD GORING: Of course it is, Father! And Chiltern has wisely accepted the government position.

LORD CAVERSHAM: I am very glad to hear that, Chiltern. Well done, sir. You will be Prime Minister one day.

[*Mason comes in.*]

MASON: Lunch is on the table, my lady. [*He goes out.*]

MABEL CHILTERN: You'll stay for lunch, Lord Caversham, won't you?

LORD CAVERSHAM: I would like that very much. And I'll drive you to Downing Street later, Chiltern. You have a great future, a great future. [*to Lord Goring*] I cannot say the same thing for you. Your place will have to be at home.

LORD GORING: Yes, Father, I prefer staying at home.

LORD CAVERSHAM: You must be good to this young lady. You must be an ideal husband. If you aren't, I won't leave you a penny.

MABEL CHILTERN: An ideal husband! Oh, I don't think I want that.

LORD CAVERSHAM: What do you want him to be then, dear?

MABEL CHILTERN: He can be what he likes. I just want to be . . . to be . . . oh! . . . a real wife to him.

LORD CAVERSHAM: That sounds very sensible.

[*They all go out except Sir Robert. He sits in a chair, thinking. After a little time Lady Chiltern returns.*]

LADY CHILTERN [*looking over the back of the chair*]: Aren't you coming in, Robert?

SIR ROBERT [*taking her hand*]: Gertrude, do you feel love for me? Or is it only pity?

LADY CHILTERN [*kissing him*]: It's love, Robert. Love, and only love. For both of us a new life is beginning.

'You must be an ideal husband. If you aren't,
I won't leave you a penny.'

ACTIVITIES

Act 1 Scenes 1–3

Before you read

1 Read the Introduction to the book. Are these sentences right or wrong? Correct the sentences that are wrong.
   - **a** This play was written after 1900.
   - **b** Wilde's mother wrote poems but he did not.
   - **c** Wilde married a woman from the United States.
   - **d** 'The Happy Prince' was a story for children.
   - **e** *Salomé* was first acted in London.
   - **f** Wilde spent three years in prison.
   - **g** He was only forty-four when he died.

2 Look at the Word List at the back of the book. Find:
   - **a** five words for people
   - **b** two parts of a play
   - **c** two things that a woman can wear

3 The title of the play is *An Ideal Husband*. What is an ideal husband? What is a perfect wife? Discuss these questions with other students.

While you read

4 Write the names.
   - **a** Who calls his son 'good-for-nothing'?   ....
   - **b** Who was at school with Mrs Cheveley?   ....
   - **c** Who has just come to England from Vienna?   ....
   - **d** Who knew Baron Arnheim a long time ago?   ....

5 Complete each sentence with one word.
   - **a** Mrs Cheveley is interested in the Argentine .... Company.
   - **b** Mrs Cheveley offers Sir Robert .... to change his mind.
   - **c** Mrs Cheveley has a .... from Sir Robert to Baron Arnheim.
   - **d** If he doesn't help her, she will tell the .... about his past.
   - **e** At the end of the scene, Sir Robert .... to do what she says.

55

6 Discuss how these people feel. Give reasons for your opinions.

    a Lady Chiltern, about Mrs Cheveley

    b Mrs Cheveley, about Lady Chiltern

    c Sir Robert, about Mrs Cheveley

    d Mrs Cheveley, about Sir Robert

Act 1 Scenes 4–6

Before you read

7 Discuss these questions.

    a What do you know about Mrs Cheveley? How can she destroy Sir Robert's work in the government? Can she even destroy his marriage?

    b Is Sir Robert really a good man? Think about his past history.

While you read

8 Number these in the correct order, 1–7.

    a Sir Robert tells his wife that he has changed his mind about the Canal Plan.   .....

    b Mabel finds a brooch on the sofa.   .....

    c Sir Robert writes a letter to Mrs Cheveley.   .....

    d Mrs Cheveley goes happily to her hotel.   .....

    e Lady Chiltern tells her husband that Mrs Cheveley was a thief at school.   .....

    f Lord Goring puts the brooch in his pocket.   .....

    g Sir Robert says that there are no secrets in his past.   .....

After you read

9 Work in pairs. Have this conversation.

    Student A: You are Lady Chiltern. You want Sir Robert to explain why he has changed his mind about the Canal Plan.

    Student B: You are Sir Robert. Talk to your wife. But you cannot tell her about the secrets in your past.

Act 2 Scenes 1–3

Before you read

10 Discuss these questions.

    a Act 2 is called 'Old Secrets'. What do you think these secrets are? Sir Robert's secrets are well known – but which other people have secrets?

    b How will Mrs Cheveley feel when she gets Sir Robert's letter? What will she do?

While you read

11 Which names complete the sentences? Write the letters A–F.

    A Baron Arnheim   B Mrs Cheveley

    C Sir Robert and Lady Chiltern   D Lord Goring

    E Sir Robert   F Lady Chiltern

    a Sir Robert can't tell his secret to his wife, but he can tell everything to ....

    b Sir Robert sold government secrets to ..... .

    c Baron Arnheim paid £110,000 to ..... .

    d Sir Robert has tried to offer money to ..... .

    e Lord Goring is a good friend to ..... .

    f Mrs Cheveley arrives and wants to speak to ..... .

After you read

12 Imagine that you are one of these people. Talk to the class.

    a You are Sir Robert. What did you do when you were a young man? Why did you do it? Are you sorry now? What did you do with the money? What kind of man are you?

    b You are Lord Goring. Are you really a lazy good-for-nothing who is never serious? Explain yourself.

Act 2 Scenes 4–5

Before you read

13 Discuss these questions.

    a Why do you think Mrs Cheveley wants to see Lady Chiltern?

    b She has received a letter from Sir Robert. What was in it?

    c What can she do now?

14 Are these sentences right (✓) or wrong (✗)?

    a Lady Chiltern has found Mrs Cheveley's brooch.   .....

    b Mrs Cheveley has always liked Lady Chiltern.   .....

    c Mrs Cheveley says that she and Sir Robert are
both dishonest.   .....

    d Lady Chiltern hears her husband's secret at last.   .....

    e Lady Chiltern feels that she can forgive her husband.   .....

    f Sir Robert feels that he has now lost everything:
his good name and his wife's love.   .....

After you read

15 Who is speaking? What do the words tell you about the speaker?

    a 'If people are dishonest once, they will be dishonest a second time. And honest people should keep away from them.'

    b 'My worst? I haven't finished with you yet.'

    c 'You seemed so good and honest. Why did I give my life to you?'

Act 3 Scenes 1–2

Before you read

16 Discuss what will happen next. Is this the end for Sir Robert? How can he stop Mrs Cheveley talking to the newspapers? Does his good name matter if his wife has stopped loving him?

While you read

17 Number these in the correct order, 1–6.

    a Lord Caversham wants his son to get married.   .....

    b Lord Goring tells Phipps that a lady is coming to
visit him.   .....

    c Mrs Cheveley finds the letter from Lady Chiltern.   .....

    d Lord Caversham arrives to talk to his son.   .....

    e Mrs Cheveley arrives to talk to Lord Goring.   .....

    f Lord Goring receives a letter from Lady Chiltern.   .....

18 Discuss these questions.

    a What does the letter from Lady Chiltern say?

    b Who is the letter to?

    c Why did she write it?

    d What does Mrs Cheveley think the letter is about?

    e What will she do with it if she can steal it?

Act 3 Scenes 3–5

Before you read

19 Discuss these questions.

    a Lord Goring thinks that Lady Chiltern is in his sitting room on a secret visit. Then Sir Robert arrives. Why is this a problem for Lord Goring?

    b The lady in the sitting room is, in fact, Mrs Cheveley, and she is listening to their conversation. Why is this a worse problem?

While you read

20 Complete each sentence with one word.

    a Lord Caversham wants to choose a .... for his son.

    b Lord Goring is very .... when Mrs Cheveley comes out of his sitting room.

    c In Lord Goring's opinion, Mrs Cheveley only loved him in the past because he was ....

    d Mrs Cheveley will give Lord Goring the letter if he will .... her.

    e Lord Goring puts the .... on Mrs Cheveley's wrist.

    f He takes the bracelet off after she gives him the ....

    g Mrs Cheveley steals the letter from Lady Chiltern. She thinks it is a .... letter.

21 Discuss these questions.
    a What does Mrs Cheveley want more than money?
    b What will Mrs Cheveley do with the letter from Lady Chiltern to Lord Goring?

22 Work in pairs. Have this conversation.
    Student A: You are Mrs Cheveley. Tell Lord Goring that you have lost a gold brooch.
    Student B: You are Lord Goring. You have the brooch. Prove that she is a thief.

Act 4 Scenes 1–4

Before you read

23 Sir Robert's good name is saved. But what will Mrs Cheveley do now? Is the 'perfect wife' in trouble?

While you read

24 Are these sentences right (✓) or wrong (✗)?
    a Mabel Chiltern and Lord Goring are in love and plan to marry.   .....
    b Lord Goring believes that Lady Chiltern's good name is now in danger.   .....
    c Sir Robert thinks that his wife's letter was sent to Lord Goring.   .....
    d Lady Chiltern thinks that her husband should now leave the government.   .....

After you read

25 How do these people feel now?
    a Sir Robert and Lady Chiltern
    b Lord Goring and Mabel Chiltern

Act 4 Scenes 5–8

Before you read

26 This is the last part of the play. Everything should end happily. Do you think:
   a that Lord Goring and Mabel will get married?
   b that Sir Robert will leave the government?

While you read

27 Write the correct names.
   a .... tells Sir Robert that the Prime Minister is offering him a position in the government.
   b .... agrees that Sir Robert should leave the government.
   c .... asks Lady Chiltern to change her mind about Sir Robert's future as a politician.
   d .... destroys Sir Robert's letter to the Prime Minister.
   e .... thinks that Lord Goring cannot be a good husband for Mabel.
   f .... tells the true story about the letter to Lord Goring.

After you read

28 Discuss how these were important to the story.
   a a gold brooch   **c** a letter without a name on it
   b a speech in the House

Writing

29 Imagine that you are a reporter. You have heard Sir Robert's speech in the House about the Argentine Canal Company. Write about it for your paper.

30 Mrs Cheveley is a terrible woman. Describe her life. What do you think she will do next?

31 Imagine that you are Sir Robert. You are going to accept the Prime Minister's offer of a position in his government. But first, write a letter to him and tell him everything about your past.

32 Imagine that you are Mabel Chiltern. You have a cousin, Emily, in the country. Write a letter to her about your life in London, and about your coming marriage to Lord Goring.

33 It is two years after the end of the play. Lord Goring and Mabel are happily married and Lord Goring has taken a position in the government. Imagine that you are Lord Caversham. Write a letter to a friend. Tell him how much your son has changed.

34 Who is your favourite character in the play? Write about him or her. Give reasons for your opinions.

35 Sir Robert wrote a letter to Baron Arnheim when he was a young man. What did he say in it? Write his letter.

36 Imagine that you are a reporter for a newspaper in 1895. You have just seen the first night of this new play by Oscar Wilde. Write about it for the theatre page of your newspaper.

37 Which actors from your country would you like to play the main parts in this play in your language? Explain why you have chosen them.

38 What changes do you need to make to the story of this play if you want to turn it into a modern play? What doesn't need to change? Give your opinions.

WORD LIST

act (n) one of the main parts of a play

ambition (n) the feeling that you want to be rich or successful

baron (n) a man with a high position in some countries because of the family he comes from

bracelet (n) something that women wear around their wrists

brooch (n) something small and pretty that women wear on a dress or shirt

canal (n) a long, narrow area of water made across land for the movement of boats

carriage (n) a passenger vehicle pulled by one or more horses

character (n) a person in a play

charming (adj) very pleasing

expect (v) to think that something will happen

ideal (adj) perfect; the best possible

lord (n) a man with a high position because of the family that he comes from

palm tree (n) a tall tree that grows in hot, dry places or near the sea

political (adj) about government activities

power (n) the ability to make decisions about other people's lives

prime minister (n) the most important person in the government in many countries which have a parliament

scene (n) a short part of a play

servant (n) someone who works in another person's house

society (n) a large group of people who live in the same area and have the same way of life. London Society was the group of rich, important people in the city.

trust (v) to believe that someone is honest